Three Native Nations

Of the Woodlands, Plains, and Desert

By John K. Manos

Illustrated by Ron Himler and
Ted Hammond

Cover: Ron Himler

Illustrations: Ron Himler and Ted Hammond

Maps: Mapping Specialists—pp. 12–13, 14–15, 22–23, 31, 34.

Photographs: Photo locators denoted as follows: Top (T), Center (C), Bottom (B), Left (L), Right (R), Background (Bkgd)

Title Page Blaine Harrington/Age Fotostock; **2** Chuck Place/Alamy; **6** Nancy Carter/ North Wind Picture Archives; **11** Philip Scalia/Alamy; **16** (B) SSPL/The Image Works, (C) Bill Frakes/Contributor/Getty Images; **17** Lawrence Migdale/Science Source; **20** (B) Blaine Harrington/Age Fotostock, (C),(R) Nancy Carter/North Wind Picture Archives; **21** (T) Fotosearch/Age Fotostock, (L) John Warburton Lee/SuperStock; **30** (Bkgd) Manuel Balce Ceneta/AP Images, (C) Glenn Asakawa/The Denver Post/ Getty Images; **34** (L) Blaine Harrington/Age Fotostock, (T) Chuck Place/Alamy; **35** Blaine Harrington/Age Fotostock; **36** (R) Mary Ellen Botter/MCT/Newscom, (BL) Macduff Everton/Corbis; **37** (B) Sylvain Grandadam/Age Fotostock, (T) Adam Woolfitt/ Robert Harding; **38** (TC) Candus Camera/Shutterstock, (R) Zuma Press, Inc/Alamy, (B) Lexine Alpert/AP Images; **39** John Cancalosi / Alamy; **40** (B) Lucas Ian Coshenet/ AP Images, (R) Dana White/PhotoEdit; **41** (bkgd) Aurora Photos/Alamy, (T) Alan Hicks/ Alamy; **44** Ernesto Burciaga/Robert Harding; **45** Joe Munroe/Hulton Archive/Getty Images; **46** Danita Delimont/Alamy.

PEARSON

ISBN-13: 978-0-328-83295-8
ISBN-10:   0-328-83295-2
5   16

Table of Contents

The Haudenosaunee
People of the Longhouse

The Birth of an Alliance

The Onondaga warriors moved as silently as shadows through the woodlands. Not even the birds were disturbed as the warriors' buckskin moccasins whispered across the ground. In a clearing were two men, Hiawatha and Deganawida, the Peacemaker. In their hands they held *wampum*, beaded belts that showed they did not come to make war. If the warriors surrounding them did them no harm, their efforts might still lead to a Great Peace.

This is part of the legend of Hiawatha. The legend explains how five native nations in what later became New York state set aside centuries of warfare to form an alliance. The five nations were the Mohawk, the Oneida, the Onondaga, the Cayuga, and the Seneca. When they joined together, they became the most powerful nation in the Northeast. They called themselves Haudenosaunee (hoe-dee-noh-SHOW-nee)—the People of the Longhouse. When French explorers and trappers met them in the 1500s, they gave these people another name: Iroquois. Their alliance became known as the Iroquois League.

Community Life

The Haudenosaunee all spoke versions of the same language and had similar ways of living. They lived in villages of longhouses, large structures with curved roofs that were covered with bark. They farmed and hunted. They had elected leaders and council meetings in their villages. Once they formed the alliance, they enjoyed a lasting time of peace and plenty.

The men were hunters and warriors—for there were still enemies outside the Haudenosaunee lands. The women were the food providers. They planted and tended the crops. They gathered nuts and fruit. Each fall, some of the crops, fruit, berries, nuts, and fish and meat were dried and buried. This would be food for the long winter.

The Three Sisters

Three plants were so important to Haudenosaunee peoples that they were called the Three Sisters: corn, squash, and beans. The Three Sisters were planted carefully. First, corn was planted in rows of small hills. Then, when the corn came up, bean and squash seeds were planted in the same mound of earth. Bean and squash plants both climb like vines. As they grew, they would wrap around the cornstalk. The Haudenosaunee gardens were easy to weed and water.

Clothing

For most of their history, the Haudenosaunee peoples made their clothes from deerskin. Women wore dresses or long shirts. Men wore hide leggings, breech cloths, and long shirts. Everyone wore deerskin moccasins. The clothes were decorated with paint, beads made of shells and wood, colored porcupine quills, and feathers.

After the Haudenosaunee came into contact with Europeans, woven cloth began to be used.

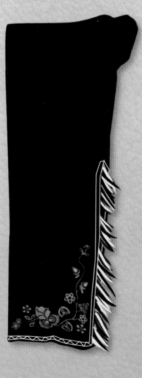

Just as important as their role providing food, women held the Haudenosaunee society together. Haudenosaunee society revolved around family groups called *ohwachira*. All of the people in an ohwachira were connected to one another through a single woman—the "mother" of the ohwachira. Usually, the oldest woman in the ohwachira was its leader. She made the important decisions for the family group.

Every village was made up of a number of longhouses. Leaders who were chosen by the clans worked together to govern the towns. Festivals and religious practices also brought the people together.

Then European explorers began to arrive.

Eagle Clan

Deer Clan

Eel Clan

Haudenosaunee Clans

Haudenosaunee society was also organized by clans. A clan was made up of two or more ohwachiras. People considered clan members to be their family. They joined the clan of their mothers. Clans had animal names and symbols, which could be seen above the door of each clan's longhouse. The head women of the ohwachiras chose the clan leaders.

The numbers of clans varied in different nations. For example, Mohawks had only three—bear, turtle, and wolf—while Senecas had eight.

Snipe Clan

Beaver Clan

Turtle Clan

Heron Clan

Bear Clan

Wolf Clan

Life in the Longhouse

The People of the Longhouse lived in wooden buildings that were about 20 feet wide and tall, and about 180 to 220 feet long. The length of a longhouse was determined by how many families lived in it. The longest ever known was 400 feet long.

Longhouses had a door at each end, and the clan symbol was above the door. There were no windows. Smoke holes in the roof let smoke from the shared fire pits escape.

The roof was curved, and the sides and roof were covered with flattened bark. Animal hides were used to seal the sides during the winter.

Inside, an aisle about 10 feet wide ran down the center of the longhouse. On either side were small sleeping booths for the families. In each booth was a raised platform. The family slept on the platform.

vents

common hall

sleeping booth

fire pit

meeting area

The longhouses were the property of the women. A longhouse was home to the family of the head of the ohwachiras in the clan. When a man and woman married, the man moved into the woman's family longhouse.

Longhouses are still important to the descendants of the Haudenosaunee. Many practice the Longhouse religion, which combines Christianity with traditional Haudenosaunee beliefs. Their meeting places are longhouses made of logs or wood frame construction, like a house.

Changes Come Quickly

Everything changed when Europeans arrived. Like all other native nations, the Haudenosaunee suffered terribly when confronted with European diseases. Smallpox, measles, influenza, and other illnesses killed thousands!

Almost as damaging, the Iroquois League became involved in European wars. France and Great Britain fought for control of the areas around the Great Lakes. The Haudenosaunee at first sided with the British against the French. Many men died during many years of war. In 1700, the Iroquois League became neutral in the conflict.

It was during this period that a related nation from the North Carolina region moved north to escape troubles with Europeans. These were the Tuscarora people. The Haudenosaunee were now six nations instead of five.

The Iroquois League was broken by the American Revolution. The Haudenosaunee government allowed individual tribes to make their own choices. The Oneidas and Tuscaroras sided with the colonists. The Mohawks, Cayugas, Senecas, and Onondagas backed the British.

When the new United States won the war, the terms of the treaty did not favor the Haudenosaunee peoples. The tribes that had sided with the British had no land in the peace agreement. They were eventually given some reservation land in Canada. This is the Grand River Reservation, the only place where the Six Nations (another name for the Iroquois League) live together today.

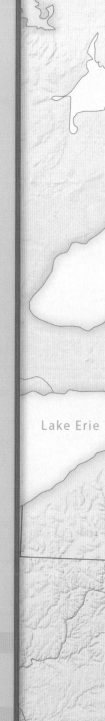

Lake Erie

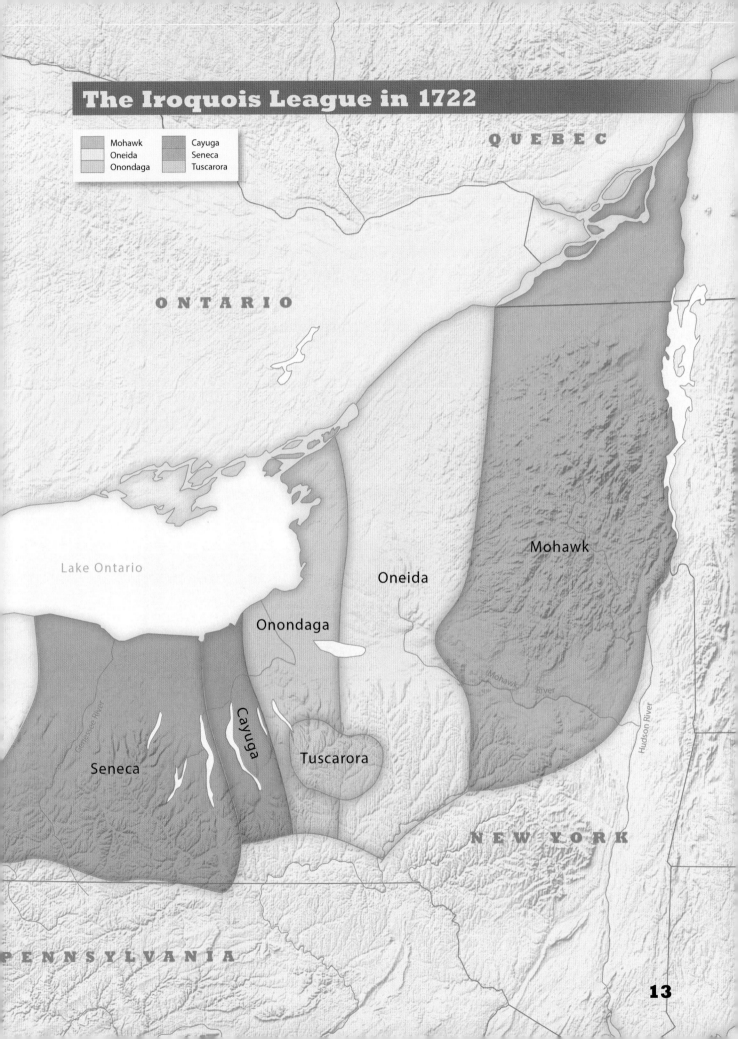

The Iroquois League in 1722

Mohawk
Oneida
Onondaga
Cayuga
Seneca
Tuscarora

QUEBEC

ONTARIO

Lake Ontario

Mohawk

Oneida

Onondaga

Genessee River

Cayuga

Tuscarora

Seneca

Mohawk River

Hudson River

NEW YORK

PENNSYLVANIA

Over time, the United States wanted New York to be open for settlers. The government took land from the remaining Haudenosaunee and forced them to move to reservations. When this happened, everything in their society began to change. Haudenosaunee men had to become farmers rather than hunters and warriors. The nations lost their land. Some were forced to move west of the Mississippi River.

As Haudenosaunee people became farmers, they stopped living in large family groups. The men replaced women as the heads of the families.

Today, Haudenosaunee people live mainly in New York, Canada, and Oklahoma. The Haudenosaunee Confederacy tries to succeed in United States society even as they struggle to hold on to their heritage.

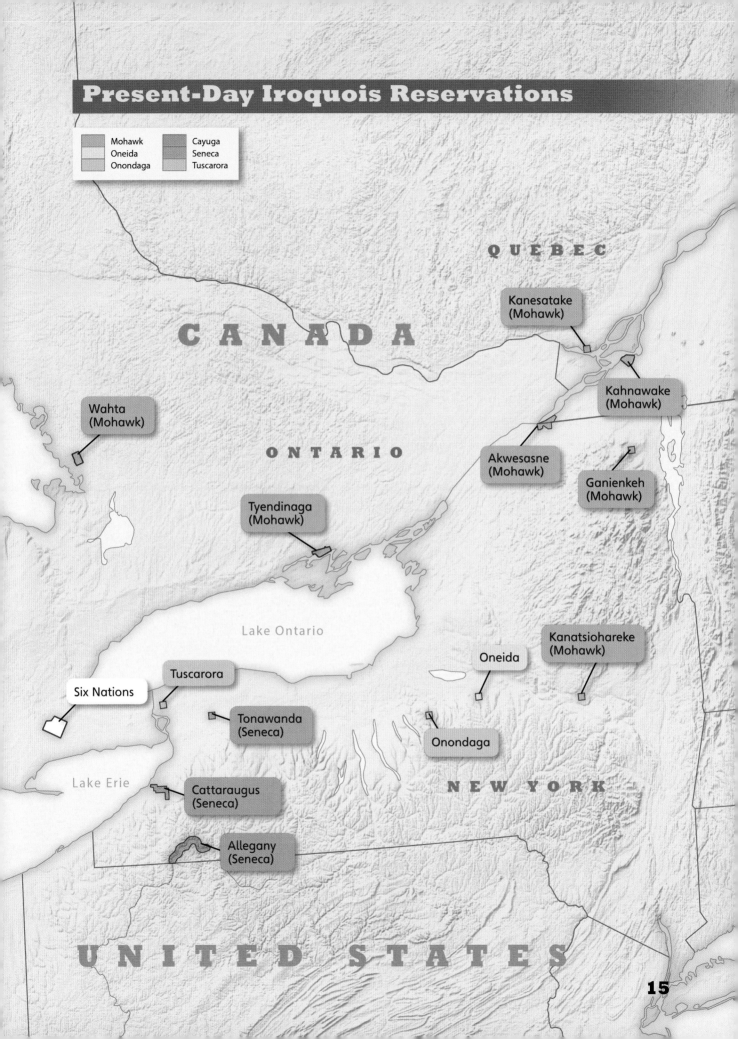

Present-Day Iroquois Reservations

Mohawk
Oneida
Onondaga
Cayuga
Seneca
Tuscarora

QUEBEC

CANADA

Kanesatake (Mohawk)

Kahnawake (Mohawk)

Wahta (Mohawk)

ONTARIO

Akwesasne (Mohawk)

Ganienkeh (Mohawk)

Tyendinaga (Mohawk)

Kanatsiohareke (Mohawk)

Lake Ontario

Oneida

Tuscarora

Six Nations

Tonawanda (Seneca)

Onondaga

Lake Erie

Cattaraugus (Seneca)

NEW YORK

Allegany (Seneca)

UNITED STATES

A Spiritual Culture—
From Masks to Sports

Haudenosaunee Spirit Faces

Masks are used in many cultures. The Haudenosaunee use two types of masks in their rituals. False Faces are carved from wood. Husk Faces are made from woven corn husks. In both cases, the faces look like spirits from the ancient stories of the Haudenosaunee.

A "Divine Gift"

The modern game of lacrosse was influenced by the Haudenosaunee hundreds of years ago. It was given its name by French explorers, who called the long stick used in the game "la crosse." The Haudenosaunee called it *tewaarathon*, which means "little brother of war." Anyone who has watched a modern-day lacrosse match knows why it was given that name!

An engraving showing the traditional Native American game of lacrosse, named so by the French settlers because of the stick's shape

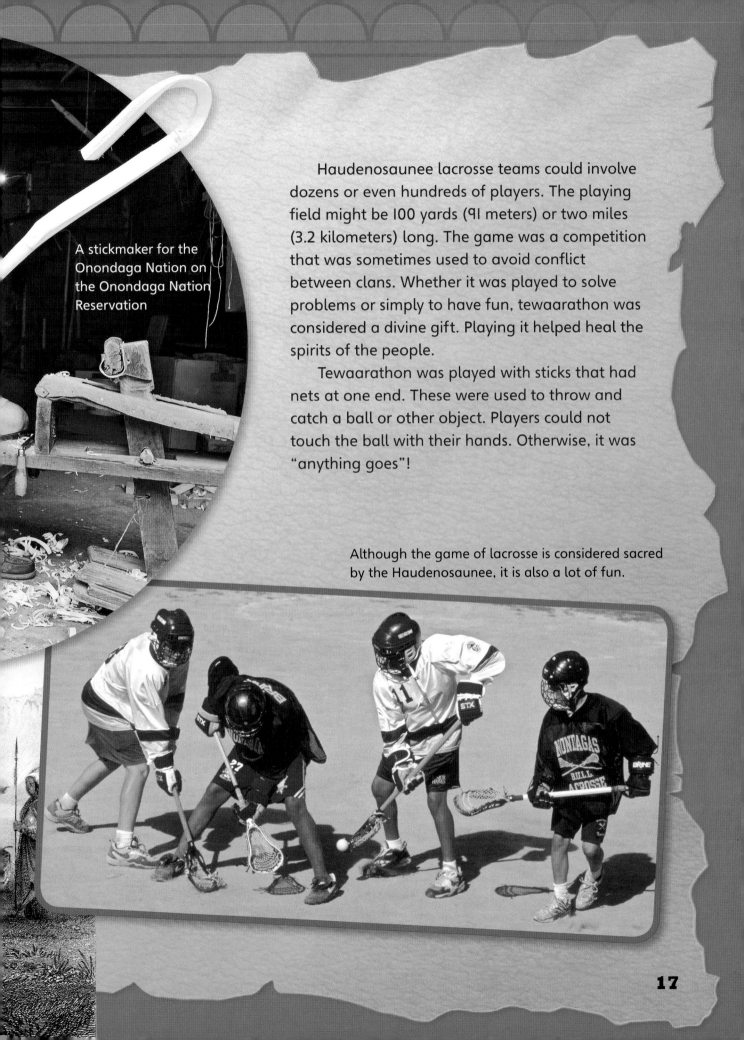

A stickmaker for the Onondaga Nation on the Onondaga Nation Reservation

Haudenosaunee lacrosse teams could involve dozens or even hundreds of players. The playing field might be 100 yards (91 meters) or two miles (3.2 kilometers) long. The game was a competition that was sometimes used to avoid conflict between clans. Whether it was played to solve problems or simply to have fun, tewaarathon was considered a divine gift. Playing it helped heal the spirits of the people.

Tewaarathon was played with sticks that had nets at one end. These were used to throw and catch a ball or other object. Players could not touch the ball with their hands. Otherwise, it was "anything goes"!

Although the game of lacrosse is considered sacred by the Haudenosaunee, it is also a lot of fun.

The Sioux
Masters of the Northern Plains

Fighting for Food— and Freedom

A fit man rides a small, tough horse. He pursues a huge, fierce bison. The bison swings its head to the side, trying to gore the horse and rider with its sharp horns.

Watching the pursuit from a hillside, a woman in a hide dress and a young boy scream encouragement. The hunter's success means life itself to the watchers on the hill.

Thanks to the pony, success is almost certain. But the hunt is still dangerous to the hunter.

Tatanka Gives Life

According to legend, before time began, the Sioux lived beneath the ground. They called themselves *Pte Oyate*, or the Buffalo Nation. But they moved to the surface of the earth. Out in the sunshine, life was difficult. The people of Pte Oyate struggled to survive.

Then a holy spirit came to them in the form of a buffalo. The spirit's name was *Tatanka*. The buffalo gave the people everything they needed to live well.

The Sioux used every part of the buffalo. The shaggy hides made blankets and warm robes when the buffalo hair was worn against a person's skin. The smooth hides were sewn together with buffalo sinew to make watertight tepee coverings. The horns made spoons and cups. The meat nourished the whole nation, while the organs were used for medicines. Buffalo hooves were boiled for glue. The bones made tools and toys.

Tepees made of buffalo hide

Parts of the buffalo were used for headdresses and clothing.

The buffalo bulls were so large and fearless that they were revered by warriors. All buffalo were deeply honored by the Sioux, who thanked the animals they killed. Each buffalo was a gift from the generous Great Spirit.

Throughout the warm months, the Sioux followed the herds of buffalo as they moved across their hunting territory. If a herd remained in one place for a number of weeks, the people would stay nearby.

A Warrior Society

The Lakota native nation, one of the peoples best known as the Sioux, fought long and hard to protect their lands and way of life. Even today, they struggle to hold on to their history and culture.

The name *Sioux*, which is most often used to describe the Lakota, is not one they gave themselves. *Sioux* comes from a Chippewa word meaning "enemy." But *Sioux* is widely used today.

The Sioux called themselves *Ociti Sakowin*, or "The Seven Council Fires." This refers to the seven groups of people who spoke different dialects of the same language.

By the 1800s, the Lakota, with their allies the Cheyenne and Arapaho peoples, were the most powerful people on the northern Great Plains. They were determined to keep their lands.

But more and more settlers crossed the continent in search of places to live. Conflict became inevitable. Yet the wars that followed were most often a result of the United States failing to honor the terms of treaties they made with the Sioux.

The Lakota were at war at times with the United States from the 1820s until their final defeats in the 1880s. The Sioux fought because treaties they signed in 1825, 1837, 1851, and 1868 were all violated by settlers.

In 1868 the Fort Laramie Treaty "guaranteed" that no whites would trespass in the Black Hills, which were the sacred heart of Lakota land. Then gold was discovered there in 1874. The final battles began. Ultimately, the Lakota were defeated and forced to move to reservations.

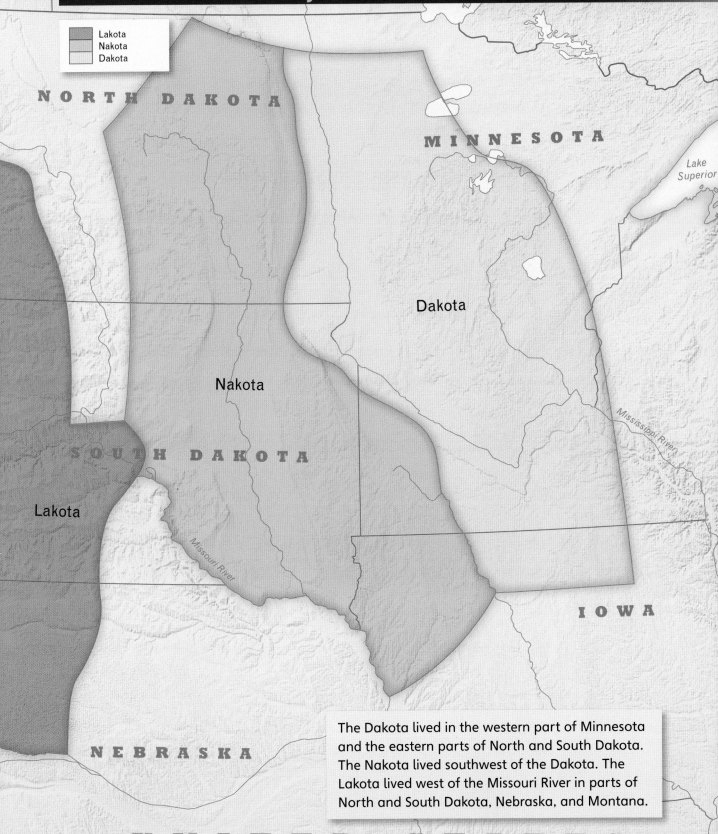

CANADA

Lakota
Nakota
Dakota

NORTH DAKOTA

MINNESOTA

Lake Superior

Dakota

Nakota

SOUTH DAKOTA

Mississippi River

Lakota

Missouri River

IOWA

NEBRASKA

The Dakota lived in the western part of Minnesota and the eastern parts of North and South Dakota. The Nakota lived southwest of the Dakota. The Lakota lived west of the Missouri River in parts of North and South Dakota, Nebraska, and Montana.

UNITED STATES

Family Life

Sioux men and women were equals, but they had different jobs in their society. The men had two main roles. They were hunters and warriors. Small groups of men worked together to hunt buffalo, deer, elk, and antelope.

War parties included larger numbers of men. Sioux warriors fought other native peoples to control hunting territories. Sometimes war parties raided other nations to steal horses.

The men also guided and protected the members of the village when they moved camps during the buffalo hunting season. During the winter, men may have made or repaired their bows, arrows, and other tools or weapons.

Women had a wider range of tasks. They removed the hides from buffalo and other animals and prepared the meat. They turned the hides into clothing, such as buffalo robes or deerskin dresses. They cut the meat into long strips and dried it in the sun. They turned buffalo hides into covers for their tepees. Women also gathered fruits and vegetables throughout the summer and fall.

The women sewed colored porcupine quills and beads into beautiful patterns on clothing. They were also responsible for packing when the group needed to move. They pulled down the tepees and loaded them onto movable platforms called travois for moving from one place to another. Then they put the tepees up again at the new camp.

Children were raised by everyone in the village. Boys played games to learn hunting skills, and they watched the herds of horses. Girls helped their mothers sew, cook, and clean, but they also played with dolls and sang with other girls. All children learned by watching their parents and listening to the stories of the elders.

The Coming of the Horse

Along with the harm caused by the arrival of Europeans, the Lakota received some things that greatly improved their lives. These benefits included metal tools and guns. But nothing improved the lives of the Lakota as much as the horse.

Horses arrived in Mexico with the Spanish. Because of their small size, these horses were called ponies. With ponies, the Lakota could travel faster and carry more goods. Their tepees could be larger. Most important of all, they could hunt buffalo more successfully. They immediately had more food and more buffalo skins.

Before the horse, the Lakota traveled with what they could carry themselves or on travois. Travois were made from poles covered with hides to make carriers for goods. After the arrival of the horse, the poles were strapped to ponies. Ponies with travois meant more dried food could be carried.

Before the horse, the Lakota struggled to survive. After the horse, they enjoyed greater wealth and power than ever before.

The Lakota, Dakota, and Nakota Today

There are more than fifteen reservations for Sioux people in the United States. The communities living on reservations are often very poor and suffer social problems. Very few of the children graduate from high school.

Many of the people have left the reservations to try to find work.

However, the Spirit Lake Nation in North Dakota has been buying land since 1960. The people there are trying to recover their traditional ways of life. The Dakota now have more than 245,000 acres of land. Wildlife, including buffalo, have been reintroduced. Children in Spirit Lake learn the Dakota language and the traditional customs and beliefs of the people.

A Lakota teacher teaches the Lakota language to high school students. This is one of the few public-school Lakota language classes in the nation.

Present-Day Sioux Reservations

Fort Peck
(Nakota, Dakota)

MONTANA

Spirit Lake
(Dakota)

Missouri River

NORTH DAKOTA

Standing Rock
(Dakota)

Lakota
Nakota
Dakota

MINNESOTA

WISCONSIN

Cheyenne River
(Lakota)

Lake Traverse
(Dakota)

Upper Sioux
(Dakota)

Prairie Island
(Dakota)

Crow Creek
(Nakota, Dakota)

Flandreau
(Dakota)

Shakopee-Mdewakanton
(Dakota)

Lower Brule
(Lakota)

Lower Sioux
(Dakota)

WYOMING

SOUTH DAKOTA

Yankton
(Nakota)

IOWA

Pine Ridge
(Lakota)

Rosebud
(Lakota)

NEBRASKA

Santee
(Dakota)

A pow-wow celebration,
Standing Rock Reservation,
North Dakota

The Pueblo Peoples
Expert Dry-Land Farmers

What's in a Name?

In 1540, a Spanish soldier at the head of a small army rode north from Mexico in search of cities of gold. What he found instead were villages of brown "apartments." The clay-brick buildings looked like stacked boxes. The Spaniards were reminded of villages back home in Spain, which they called "pueblos."

This is how the Pueblo peoples received the name that they are commonly called.

The Pueblo once lived all across what is now New Mexico and Arizona, plus parts of southern Utah, southern Colorado, northern Mexico, and western Texas. Now they live mainly in New Mexico.

There are nineteen Pueblo groups in New Mexico. Many of these groups are found along the Rio Grande and its tributaries. One, the Taos Pueblo in Taos, New Mexico, has lived there for about one thousand years. The groups share their ancestors' lifestyles and religion. But the groups are separate from one another. Some are quite different in their customs.

Nineteen Pueblo Communities

Today's nineteen Pueblo groups are shown on the map of northern New Mexico. The Hopi people are a Pueblo nation, but they occupy their own reservation in Arizona.

A Zuni Pueblo man in full regalia

A ceremonial Laguna Pueblo dance

COLORADO

Taos

Picuris

Santa Clara

Ohkay Owingeh
Pojoaque

San Ildefonso

Nambe

Jemez

Tesuque

Zia

Cochiti

Santo Domingo

San Felipe

Santa Ana

Sandia

Laguna

Rio Puerco

ARIZONA

Laguna

Zuni

Laguna

Isleta

Acoma

Zuni River

Laguna

Zuni

Little Colorado R.

NEW MEXICO

Rio Grande

Rio Chama

Pecos River

A Zuni Pueblo ceremony

Life in the Desert

What the native nations of the Southwest accomplished is almost hard to believe. Without huge dams to provide irrigation, some of them farmed the desert. They built cities and thrived in one of the harshest environments in North America.

The farming methods of the Pueblo peoples—the Pueblos, Zunis, and Hopis—are worth mimicking today. They have been proved by the test of time. The Pueblo have lived in those dry lands for at least 1,500 years.

Long ago these people learned what crops could be planted in the lands that they call home. They learned how to bring water to their crops in dry years. They are able to preserve their food by drying it for storage. They are perfectly adapted to the deserts of the Southwest.

They still plant fields of corn, beans, and squash. They still fashion jewelry using silver and turquoise. They also still weave baskets and form pots from clay. In many ways the Pueblo peoples have maintained their ancient ways of life.

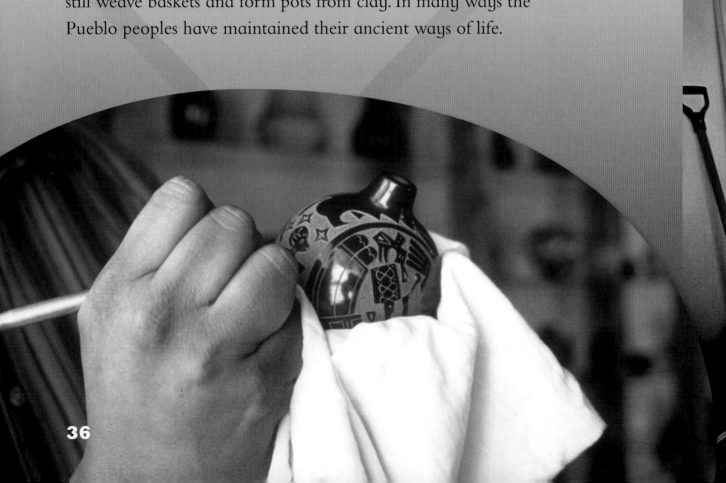

Food in a Dry Climate

The Pueblo today farm as their ancestors did. They dig deep holes with planting sticks. One seed goes in each hole, which may be twelve or fourteen inches deep. The holes are deep so that the seeds may reach some ground moisture.

The seeds are planted on slopes to catch whatever infrequent rain may fall. Sometimes a small mound of dirt is raised around each hole to catch rain. The Pueblos also build small dams across streams to catch water for irrigation.

Ancestors of the Pueblo harvested wild plants such as turnips and spinach, but the crops were mostly corn, beans, and squash. Still today the Pueblo use several different colors of corn.

Corn was their staple. Bread was baked in a hole in the ground that was covered with hot stones. One thing the Pueblos adopted from the Spanish was a round outdoor bread oven used by the whole village.

Men and boys hunted for small game such as rabbits and ground squirrels. Only the men pursued larger animals, such as deer, bison, and bighorn sheep.

Unloading blue corn to be milled, Santa Ana Pueblo, New Mexico

Harvesting carrots,
Taos Pueblo, New Mexico

Preparing land for planting
native crops, Albuquerque,
New Mexico

Family Life

Clans dominated village life. These were large family groups that were headed by women. Women also owned the property in Pueblo society. The clans took their names from nature—Eagle Clan, Corn Clan, and so on. A man married into his wife's clan. Children were born into their mother's clan.

Boys and girls had different jobs that prepared them for adult life. The boys learned to hunt and irrigate crops. They learned to plant and raise the crops as well. They also were taught how to weave cloth.

Girls were taught how to cook, grind corn, preserve food by drying it, and make pottery.

Many Pueblo people continue to practice their old religion. Every Pueblo village has at least two *kivas*. A kiva is an underground room that is used for religious ceremonies.

The Pueblos build their homes of adobe brick and stone. Like their ancestors, they mix sand, clay, and water together in rectangular blocks. These dry and become very hard. The adobes are the basis of their buildings. Often, their homes were built one on top of another. The floor above was set back so that the top of one room was like the patio for the next level up.

Kivas

The underground chambers called *kivas* were sometimes as large as one hundred feet across. The kiva included a fire pit and a *sipapu*. A sipapu was a small hole in the ground symbolizing the opening through which ancient ancestors first came into the world, according to legend. Most of the time, only men went into the kivas through a hole in the roof.

In some ceremonies, *kachinas*—friendly spirits—were honored. This is true for Zuni and Hopi ceremonies today as it was long ago. The kachinas may be spirits of people, animals, or even plants. In the ceremonies men may dress as kachinas and come up out of the kivas to dance.

No windows were used on the ground level. The only way into the apartments was through a hole in the roof. The people climbed ladders to get to their homes. When the ladders were pulled up, they could not be attacked.

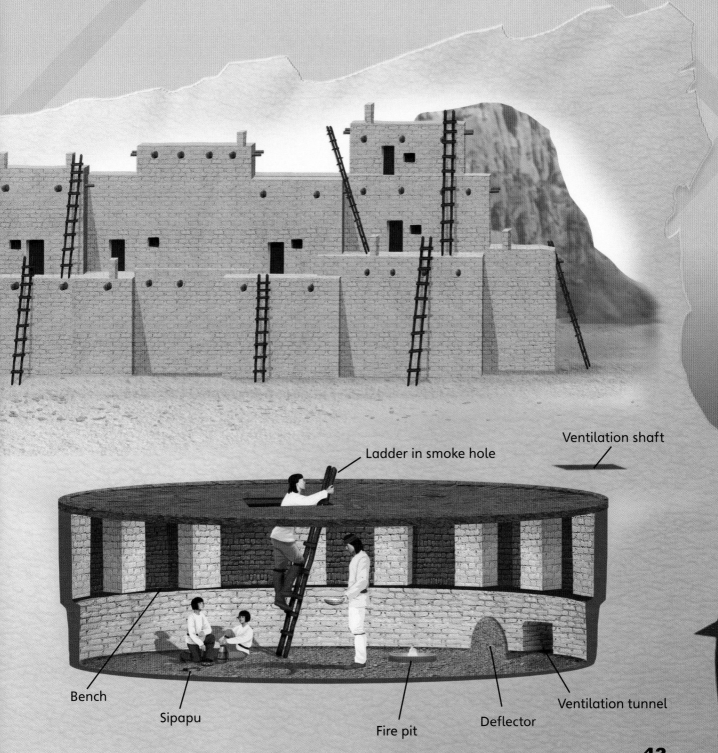

Ventilation shaft

Ladder in smoke hole

Bench

Sipapu

Fire pit

Deflector

Ventilation tunnel

Contact with Spaniards

Spanish explorers arrived in what is now New Mexico in 1540. They had a battle with a Zuni village where they stole some food.

Some of the things the Spanish brought were useful. The Pueblos made use of metal and domestic animals such as horses, sheep, and chickens. The wheat, grapes, and other fruit the Spaniards planted were welcome. But the Spanish also brought European diseases. These diseases killed most of the inhabitants of many Pueblo communities. Many of the survivors were forced to abandon their villages.

Missionaries arrived with the Spanish. They demanded that the Pueblo stop practicing their own religion. Some of the Spanish wanted to make slaves of the Pueblo. In 1680, the Pueblo people rebelled. They were able to drive the Spanish back to Mexico. This was one of the few real victories for any Native Americans. No Europeans returned until 1692.

The Pueblo peoples have a long and proud history. They have faced many challenges, but they continue to draw strength from their traditions and rich culture. They are a thriving community in the 21st century.

Pueblo Arts

Men weave cloth in many patterns.

Pueblo pottery is made by the women.

Kachina dolls look like the kachinas of religious ceremonies.

Glossary

alliance agreement between two groups of people to support one another in war

breech cloths wide strips of cloth or hide worn between the legs and held in place with a belt

buckskin softened deer hide used to make clothing

clan group of related people

confederacy group of nations or states that have joined together with an agreed set of rules

descendants people with a common ancestor

dialects different forms of the same language, such as different pronunciations of the same words

irrigation method of bringing water to crops

mimicking copying; doing the same thing as

nourished fed in a healthy way; helped to maintain life

revered held in great respect

sinew fibers from animal muscles; tendons

treaties agreements between two nations or groups of people to settle differences

tributaries smaller streams that flow into rivers

Index